THE ONLY WORLDS
WE KNOW

THE ONLY WORLDS WE KNOW

Michael Lee

—

Published by Button Poetry / Exploding Pinecone Press
Minneapolis, MN 55403 | http://www.buttonpoetry.com

—

Cover design: Nikki Clark

ISBN - 978-1-943735-60-0

23 22 21 20 19   1 2 3 4 5

til mor og far og fedrelandet

TABLE OF CONTENTS

V

what's a little more pain
when pain's eternal?

—MATT RASMUSSEN

I

AND

what does it mean
when you and your love sleep

in the same bed for the last time
& you lie awake saying nothing

because you know it
& maybe if you never

sleep you will never
wake & the birds

won't sing & the sun
won't know to rise & you

won't ever be alone again. & what
does it mean when you can feel

her body only a foot from your own,
but you are certain if you reached

out for her arm or cheek
you would not find anything

other than the sheets, still warm,
& no matter how close she gets

to you now, she will always be out of reach.
& what does it mean when, finally,

you fall asleep & both awaken
to a gunshot in the dark—

like a single string
in the instrument of night

had snapped—
& she crawls into your arms

for protection—but of course not the real kind,
because that bullet, if aimed at you,

would have gone through you both—
what does it mean when you realize

that's all love is: a small & feeble shelter
from the inevitable?

From bullets & time,
from rain & also drought,

& if the bullet were just a tool of grammar
in the language of the unspeakable,

would it not be a conjunction,
would it not be the word "and"

for doesn't it connect us
to the only two worlds we know?

THE LAW OF HALVES AS APPLIED TO THE BLADE

2.

My math teacher steps
toward the blackboard proving
that if you continue to halve
a distance between two points
you will never reach the end.

1.

I stood two feet from the door.
Then one foot. Then six inches.

.5

From the onset of forward motion, the knife
must have been two feet from the first point of entry.
I picture it being one foot. Then six inches.

.25

The knife is barely moving now.
Its point still hovers over his chest.
His shirt is clean and his hair dry, and I
have grown older waiting for him to return.

.125

He has had time to ask his mother why.
She has had time to notice his new haircut.
His laughter thawing in the air.
The basketball spinning forever in his hands.

.0625

There are still, in the end, atoms shivering
between us. In this way none of us ever
really touch, and the blade hovers there
forever, and my hand never slides
across his casket or holds the morning
paper hot with his name. Even now
I feel his face warm against mine,
wet with laughter or perhaps

0.

HUM

The fly suspects I'll be dead soon—
some nights I suspect the same.

It hovers, touching me lightly
before lifting off surprised, as I am,

by my warmth. It is a kind of madness
to see the inevitable and be unable stop it

or even articulate its reach, to reach
and be made of so many small failures:

this buzzing I cannot kill. I cannot leave.
I cannot touch the ones I love

made small by love.
I try to resurrect you here—

where you live now—on the haggard wings
of memory. I fail, and close my eyes,

and fail there too. No one even has a face,
and still I set the table. No one is coming.

No one becomes someone I knew
once. I feed its absence and it grows

and all the gone things continue
to go. I knock and knock on the walls

of my home, and No One answers.
I swear, I swear if I touch this wall

again a door will burn red
in the middle.

.

SELF-ERASURE AS APPLIED TO MY MEMORY

24.

It was the season of ghosts locked
in the windowpanes and the cellar lamp,
the grindstone abandoned amongst the coal
generation after generation. It was the year
the abandoned house down the block burned
to the ground and another fell into itself
and both sprouted into strange mansions
with ghostless windows and storyless attics.
My grandmother became the bed sheets, though thinner
than the bed sheets, until she vanished
like the words "I love you" just hours after
I last said them. Sometimes, I believe I had
given her permission to go—my ego tells me this.
It was the year the ego grew legs and made
things tumble and burn. It was the year
I didn't sleep, but could not leave my bed.
It was the year of vanishing
which I had learned from the dead.
It was the year I became the pipe,
then the couch, and then the air as it whistled
through my bones like a bolt. It was the year
I did not eat unless it was the moonlight or
the blue light of the television. It was the year
I did not dream and spoke only in curses.
It was the year magic fell dead in the street
like a struck crow and darkened beneath
the cars as they left and kept leaving.
That year my friend was murdered, and though
I can remember his laugh, and his hair—

how it came to a widow's peak, his afro
a curled crown—I recall nothing else, not his eyes
or his body, and now barely his smile.
That year, my grandfather also died.
I can remember him shaving, but I cannot
recall his face or the hair that must have been there.
That year the crops, which had not been grown
on our land for a hundred years, came up
through the floorboards and from the faucets,
and all of our mouths were full of grain, and corn,
and drought, and shadows. It was the year
I lived on a train and passed the rusted shipyards
outside of New York heading into Connecticut.
The train burned and burned like a whistle and drove
straight into the sea. That year, from the windows which
I guarded like a ghost, I watched someone else's
grandfather feeding his cat on the countryside; the man
gazed out onto the horizon as though
he noticed just then half his life was missing
from his memory. I am told that it too was the year
I was dying. I would sleep on the kitchen floor
after each meal, a plug of tobacco tucked gently
into my lip as though it were a thing that could wake
or wake something in me. Some dream seed
rupturing in the mouth. I don't remember this,
it is a false memory, it is the image of the Mona Lisa
as described to you by the janitor of the Louvre,
and though he or she knows the painting best—
the coy look of mischief, the conquering nature
of the eyes—without seeing it, that image is not yours,
or even mine, just as each story that has ever been told is
hardly a replica of light. It was the year
I remembered and remembered and remembered,

the act of remembering like sharpening a blade until
the blade is gone. Only a hilt now. Only nothing.
It was the year when I was twenty-four or maybe twelve
but probably six, it was the year in which all years
became the same, and my whole life existed in a single
dream fading away, a block of salt worn by rain,
drop by drop.

OUT THERE

He went back out, the sentence

                         sounds just like that,

                                a sentence

to death and misery

                     or the desire   for misery.

I have sentenced myself yes,

                                many times

to die. The pills swelling

                                like a fist

full of little white pupils in awe

of what they can do   in the body.

If I am alive now it is because

of how many times   I have failed.

My first night clean, I wasn't.

                           I threw up in the street

and stumbled in late. An old man,

                              sober thirty years, said,

Give it six months. If you don't like it,

                     you can have all your pain

                              and misery back.

             • • •

But it was mine, it was mine
and I could make as much of it as I needed.

             • • •

How much liquor can the body hold
until the body leaves itself behind?

Each week, a new man enters
the room, each week another man doesn't

come back. What magic, to walk through
a door and then appear again as ink

in the Sunday paper. *He went back out,*
the sentence, a sentence, spoken so often

it becomes a single word, an incantation
of disappearance, a spell, the addict

a magician after all, and you wonder
where all these men have gone, but you don't

you know.

　　　• • •

You know there is no long winter *out there*
　　　　　where we dig through dead pines

in search of the bottom.
　　　　　Pain, another way to fly.
　　　　　　　Misery, another way to vanish.

Misery, the prettiest word.
　　　　　It flutters on the tongue
　　　　　　　like sonata, like overture,

like other words that carry us
　　　　　into the dark and then beyond it.

　　　　　• • •

Ten years ago I entered a room full of men
sitting quietly as if they had been waiting

for the last open chair to fill.
Now more than half of them are dead.

What's a little more pain
                    when pain's eternal?

What's a little more music
                    when the skull is a bell?

What's a little more knocking
                    against its walls

when the body is a cathedral of doors
through which all the angels have already fled?

Listen, can you hear it?

                    Out there?

                              The wind aching?

The goldenrod reaching up

                    through the snow,

where every house is a church,

                    and you are never cold,

the dead are just barely beyond

                    what you can touch,

and every life you could have had sings.

II

THE STUDY OF KNIVES AND MUSIC

The knife is envious of bones, each metatarsal
of the foot, collar and jaw, but especially the rib

and its motionless rest. The knife
remembers when it was bone, when it lived

inside an elk or man and kept the rind
together until it didn't, until the body

was used against itself. Do you see how
everything returns to its maker? The way, at its end,

an elephant remembers where it once rose
like grey light from the earth—its bones cutting

through the hide—a moonlit sculpture unearthed
by the sharp arms of the clock as they swing

at the flank. The sunlight enters, guiding the flies,
and their rhythmless chatter as if death were a kind

of realization the body has.
Where else do you expect the knife to go

other than back inside us? Here, beside the heart,
where it sleeps like a tucked wing.

•

The knife falls
needle on record

the LP spins
backward, sound

siphoned
from vinyl

the disc wiped
clean

the music shakes
inside the amplifier

his body begins
to unravel

in the arms
of a clock

blood unspooled
his body returns

cotton drifting
skyward.

The wind
gathers seeds.

·

The phone falls from his hand, though
remains on. The moment of his death lives

now in his cousin's right ear and in the wires
between them. Every sneaker strung

over the lines from Palo Alto to Minneapolis
fell to the ground. Another murder

of crows, perched along the line,
felt his voice unhinge from his throat

and rifle through the sky,
but they did not hear it. This language

of grief is not a spoken language.
The only song that can be written

in its tongue is no song at all,
is morning, is traffic before it is traffic

when three hundred million cars
across America sleep and somewhere,

east of everything I know, dawn
opens, a red fist unlatching.

THE INSOMNIAC MAPS THE NIGHT

A group of dead friends is called
a memory. A grouping of grave robbers,

a scalpel. I know of a surgery
that removes nothing,

rearranges each vertebra
into a necklace

of names speaking into the dark
asking me to join them,

to let the night wear me
thin. Each second

a lathe, ground me down
until I knew the the exact hour

in which traffic is born,
and in which I am

most likely to consider running
this coin-thin light across my neck.

I have found the hour
in which my dead friends congregate

and knock against my head,
laughing, bouncing a basketball

against the door. One points
to the last hour of good light,

and, as I begin to lace my shoes, says,
hurry up. Open the door. Just open it.

INDIFFERENCE

I've stared out a second-story window all day
through the soft falling of snow
and the intermittent rumble of truck engines

outside the granary. I've sat alone
on the stage of an empty theater at midnight
and played the piano, poorly, for no one at all.

I sat in the last row and watched the stage
lights, the dust hovering beneath them,
and the musty curtains do nothing at all

for no one. I've turned on the lights
of the marquee in a small Minnesota town
standing before the empty theater, above which

I briefly lived, until a single bulb flickered out
like a firefly in rain. I walked the river
and the steel bridge at night. I rested beside

the dam and felt as insignificant as its mist,
and in this way, briefly free. What was each brick
in that town if not indifferent to my wandering

in its dim light, and what is indifference
if not a kind of violence we must each survive
but won't. The indifference of crows and water.

The indifference of bluffs and deer crossing
the highway at night. The indifference of cities
and of clocks. The indifference of our own blood

whirring like a mill wheel inside us
where death is always monotonous.
The heart stops and that's the end of it.

SOUND LOST IN THE NORTH

And there, the light clank and moan
of the wind chimes spread out across the garden.

An unexplained crack in a windshield, frost
across a pane of glass, you could watch it all

at once. Minnesota winter is like that:
far enough north and you have to strain to hear

a distant rifle, especially if it finds its mark—
the sound disappears with the bullet into the meat.

I've known nights so cold the body is unlikely
to bleed. I have braved my own heart and swung

a hammer so honestly that smoke curled off
the nail. Still there was no sound. Each moment

of winter is so faint and silent it is a memory
even as you live it. And so it was then

as the hammer fell with such repetition it became slow
and soft, like snow, falling again and again

and again until the birds froze mid-song
and the wordless chimes swayed like dark ropes.

ERASURE   APPLIED TO MY MEMORY

12.

It was the season of ghosts
in the wind   and the
                    abandoned   coal
generation after generation
the   house   burned
to the ground   fell into itself
and   sprouted   strange
        ghostless windows a   storyless attic
My grandmother became   thinner
than
        the words
                                        I had
given her   my ego tells me
It was the year the ego   made
things   burn. It was the year
I didn't   leave my bed.
It was the year of vanishing

        the year I became the pipe,
                        then the air as it whistled
through   the year
I did not eat
                            It was the year
I did not dream and spoke only in curses.
                magic fell dead in the street
                        and darkened
                        and kept leaving.
That year my friend was murdered
                    his laugh   his hair

I recall nothing else

That year, my grandfather   died
                              shaving, but I cannot
recall his face   that must have been there.
That year
                    a hundred years came
                              from the faucets,
and all of our mouths were full of
      drought and shadows. It was the year
I lived

                    and burned like
            the sea.
        like a ghost
          feeding
            the horizon

      his memory

                    as though it were a
                              dream

        described   by the janitor of   Lo v e,
      and
                    mischief

                    each story that has ever been told is
      hardly   light.

the act of remembering   sharpening   until
                      nothing
It was the year when I was   or maybe
but probably   it was the year in which all years
became the same, and my whole life existed in a single
dream   worn by rain

THE PILL

a small moon or bomb
which kills no one

quickly, dissolves like a moment
over time and never

completely. The pill, a tooth
of light, enters the body.

A blinding seed tears open
the dark of me, hot lash

of lightning splitting the sky,
a zipper across a black bag.

The pill infinite.
The pill a solar system

in the dead man's eye. The pill
a white shadow dragging night

behind it; I reached so far
into the medicine cabinet

my hand came back out
through my mouth. I looked

into the mirror for so long I forgot
who I was. Introduced myself,

tried to say my name, but instead a fist
swung like a curse and shattered the glass.

THE STUDY OF WORDS AND HEAVEN

Given that the etymological opposite of *remember*
is not actually *forget*, but is in fact *dismember*,

I ask you now to consider that we've been reading
Mary Shelley's Frankenstein all wrong:

the Dr.'s patchwork monster was remembered
to life and so is this not an allegory

for the ways in which our memories betray us?
Is it true if I remember a dead boy one thousand

different ways, a thousand new boys will rise
from my mouth? Will the sea give him back?

Do you recall when the Bill of Boyhood was passed,
requiring that all ash gathered be remembered

into fire and such flame be returned
to wood with which we rebuilt our childhood

homes as we remembered them? And so
they were, of course, erected backward.

Many jagged, some built upside down,
some with parents where there were none,

some with food and not hunger, some
with grandparents and not ghosts.

By what artifice are we held
together? What is the difference

between memory and dream?
For which is it appropriate to grieve?

If both were a kind of kindling,
which might you suggest we burn?

•

Child becoming smoke.
Child becoming the morning

newspaper, I burned
each page and watched

the words curl in the dark
wind. Angel-faced boy,

the kind of face saints
line up to name.

•

Once I knew a boy
with a face that was a kind

of heaven. It held the dead
and the dreams of the dead,

which is to say it held him,
and his dreams. And if I go

here, to the face of heaven
when I go, St. Peter will stand

at his teeth, as always, only a few
endless inches beneath those

even more endless eyes. Endless
when they were a brown deep as earth.

Endless now because they are filled
with earth, and what does the earth see

but everything? What is the earth
but a single massive eye? Ask me

where I'll go when I go and I'll say
that face the size of the sky.

.

Once a year I wear your jacket
and listen to the 67 cents jingling

in the pocket. I should tell you
it has bought me nothing—not sleep

nor dreams nor peace, not even
a single tooth trapped in your smile

trapped in your face, trapped behind
the nine o'clock television screen.

.

When you were killed, I began
to write letters to my own murderer.
I dropped them off at the post office
with no address. Now, in my 30th year,
one by one by one at my doorstep.
What a terrible magic, the day
we find out who we really are.

CERTAINTY

This apartment now
       with no one in it,

only the sky forcing
       its way through

the screens, me, the wind,
       a single mouse

chattering away until the trap
       closes its copper mouth.

The neighbors screaming,
       screaming, something

about *a knife,*   *a knife.*
       I know this song,

I think, each letter extends
       almost to the brink

until the sound nearly runs out,
       but it is there still,

almost still, a whisper caught
       on the window sill,

that word so many times,
       like a secret

password to some door,
      a secret knock,

the way all secrets work
      against the body,

demanding entry,
      and then

ROW

The boat fills with water as we cross
the wide lake. You bail with a cracked
bucket while I row. We both laugh,

      guided by the campfire burning on
      the distant shore made of driftwood,
      another boat we found smashed among

the rocks. Wood lapping against stone,
a kind of laughter in its own way. I think,
in this moment, of my name,

      of that song the church ladies sang to me
      about rowing my boat to shore before
      I had been to enough funerals to swear

off church for good. Though somehow I find
myself praying through my laughter as the water
gathers around my ankles. I try it sometimes,

      prayer that is, in secret but I keep noticing
      I'm doing it. Look, I've caught myself.
      I'm not even a half decent non-believer.

Every adventure is a creative new way to die;
I keep on living despite. I can't ever seem
to get it right. Once my skin crackled electric

      and a god got wedged in my skull, I tried
      to leap out a window and join him. I woke
      handcuffed to a gurney, my jaw wired shut

by what I saw and could not say. Of course
I smoked up the next day. Of course I took the pills
and then woke and kept waking. I huffed the vapor

    and collapsed and kept on rising
    in my stupid and simple way. Fuck it.
    In my favorite dream I row that boat forever;

the fire finds its way inside me.
I've been clean for ten years, sometimes
barely. I could throw it away if I wanted

    and in my favorite dreams I do. I want. I give up
    and the water is so goddamn cold it keeps me
    alive forever, which is another way of dying

again and again and never quite being dead.
And that's the horror of life. The water
so green it shatters my sternum and there

    a single glowing stone. I want it in my palm,
    to make it skip and crackle like a rat scratching
    away in the vein. I laugh and I wake up laughing

and I want. I simply want and what dear god
is on the other side of want? I want that too.
My want is so wide I cannot cross it.

TAPESTRY IN FIVE PARTS

•

Driving north through Minnesota
in winter, our family car without heat,
the passenger door held shut with rope.

My sisters and I in our snowsuits, squeezed
into sleeping bags and buckled tightly in
the back seat. It is the closest we will ever be.

•

The abandoned house down the street
burning to the ground. The neighbor boys
and I cheer in its thundering light.

A firefighter is dragged from the house.
Laid, unmoving, in the street. We tell
ourselves he's still alive and continue.

•

In the field beside the ashen ruins
of that abandoned house, farm equipment

unused since the neighborhood was a farm,
a rusted plow the color of embers and clay.

New machines make everything
into dirt. Then slowly a cul-de-sac,

five mansions begin to form
and finish the work of the fire.

·

My friend sits in his car nearby while I grapple
with a boy on the sidewalk. I am on top,
punching him in the face. My friend, laughing,

on three tabs of acid, cranks classical radio
and cheers as he narrates every swing. I continue.
An aria. Snow falls. I continue. Working.

Diligently. Like fire. A machine. Making
heat where there is no heat. Somewhere else,
more laughter. Perhaps it is mine.

·

It's winter, still. Always. Somehow.
I am above the soil by luck at this point.

My friend next door is wheeled from
her house beneath a white sheet. Her

husband, home from rehab that morning,
sits shivering on the front steps and says

nothing. We go to a 12-step meeting
that evening. He helps me change

my tire. We pretend we are friends too.
He asks how to stop it. Years later

he will drink himself to death, and I will
hold a pistol in my hand and wonder.

NEW YEAR'S EVE, 2015

Spike is still dead, Don too. The dirt across Space-
man's grave is fresh, and empty, and the last
thing I said to him was to shut the fuck up.
I meant it. Two nights later he did. Closed
his mouth around as many pills as he could
fit in his palm and never opened it again.
I told him we'd get coffee this winter. It's winter
now, I swear I meant that too. I've had enough
for the both of us and cannot sleep.
Time unravels into mist across the Atlantic,
and I know the next year has come
bearing the world in its palms like wet fruit
when the gunfire wakes the dark and the snow
comes slowly down a little more after each *clack*
like it's been stuck up there all year.
As a boy, I didn't understand why my uncle
ran out into the snow in his long underwear
just in time to unload his .40 upward
through the needles of the pines,
but I understood he missed his father,
and I have always understood snow.
Each bullet pleads for the dark to just
let go. That's all this is, shooting the sky
a kind of demand: *Give us back those we love,*
open up and let me take back the things
I said or never said drifting across
the frozen lake and the silent boulevards.
Heaven is so stingy, and there are so few
snowflakes fluttering passed the streetlamps
that if they were pills I could not kill myself.
If they were pills, I'd probably try anyway.

I'll try anything that doesn't work
because it might. My faith is so thin now
it could slip by me as easy as a whole year.
I don't own a gun because I'd use it. I don't
shoot anything anymore. I don't pray either—
what's the difference and what's the use?
I'd free everyone or join them. Let me in
god, my god let me out of here. Each bullet
is a single knuckle rapping upon the tomb
of the world and there are bodies on both sides.
Which is mine, O lord, which is mine?

LEAVING

Clean the way a fly is clean or the way a wound is
clean, and a maggot is clean and cleaning,
the city clean as a casket before the body

is placed like a pill inside of it.
Clean as a pipe washed white
by fire. When I was a boy I cursed

so much my mother scrubbed my mouth
with soap, and now what curses do I have
left to clean the dead?

When I left, I drove east
in a car painted the same color as my luck,
out of Minneapolis where the road opens

like a stone tulip into all other roads. My last sight
of home, a man I knew once driving beside me.
When I saw him I saw he did not see,

but was a kind of sight—nothing like the man
I once knew, but more like the clothes
this man will one day leave behind when he goes.

Last I heard, he had already gone, guided
by the winding fingers of meth and its nails
made of smoke. What can I say now but nothing?

What can I say as I head east and all I hear
is a dark rattling trailing me like wedding cans
for the marriage of dirt and rain?

What can I say as I pass through
Wisconsin's endlessly green and stupid fields
and come upon a car cleaved in two?

The bodies it had carried litter the highway
like salt. What a beautiful day to leave home
and let your mouth hang open.

What can I say as I pass torn up highway after highway
riddled with skeleton crews? In the right light
this thoroughfare looks like a glimmering bone.

I mean a dark breeze ridden with flies,
heat cooking the meat straight from the ribs
of deer along I-94 like dead lanterns leading me home.

Home? To what now? To dirt? To glass? To wind
hollow as a skull and the summer caught
inside of it. Somewhere there is a classroom

comprised of all my dead friends—
as they were once—pledging allegiance
to a Polaroid developing forever.

If old age is not defined by time but by one's proximity
to death then I grew up with a group of 13-year olds
who were a thousand years each.

Let us sit together now at this table of holy oak—
let us eat well on all we do not have the words
to describe. Please, pass the gun metal and salt.

Let me preserve this documentation of ruin.
Some nights, I want to stay this way forever.
I want to sing until the grass sews my mouth shut.

What is the exact key of an instrument decomposing
beneath the dirt? Every road east is a single thread
in America's long taxonomy of pain. There is no word

for a journey comprised entirely of leaving.
What left was there to do but go on
driving east with everything I owned,

passed an endless field of sunflowers,
a 100-mile stretch of yard sales. An 88
Cutlass, grandma's jewelry, a hickory cabinet.

God, if I could make money off this memory
I might just give you everything.

6.

It was the season of ghost
        wind   and
                                                coal

the   house   burned
to the ground
and   sprouted
                                storyless

        words

I didn't

                vanish

                I became the pipe
                        then the air

I did not eat
                                                the
        dream   only   curses
                                dead
                                dark
                        and   leaving.
That year   was murdered

That year

came
from the faucets

and burned

AT THE LAKE

you will never touch again,
I offer myself myself,
reach to sever the same water
by which I am severed, hewn
by the wide blue blade.
Only my shadow touches
land, the shadow its own
departure, the way light
is the only witness to
what it touches and cannot
itself be seen. Only what it illuminates:
a single sparrow studying
nightfall, learning nothing
about nothing until its body,
and song—its most dedicated
scholarship—are gone. Still
in their absence, there was a boy
and then there wasn't.
His shadow broke free
like a single witness refusing
to witness anymore, running
darkly away, the shadow
so light on its feet it seems
we would call it flight
if it would simply lift off the hot grass.
The shadow is everything
removed, the shadow is proof
of what light cannot do
and what terrible things
we have done beneath it.

IV

THE STUDY OF THE DEAD AND PUZZLES

The knife does not kill the body, it simply informs it
that death is possible: a sudden light flooding the room,
the one corner of the house we never knew

existed until all other rooms had darkened. Once
I saw myself in a storefront's glass and felt lost
somewhere in the middle, a single word stuck

between two people. I wondered
if dying would be as simple as shattering
a window. I knelt beside the lake and drank

the water for I was in it. This is how the body
misinterprets thirst. I knew a man who drank himself
to death. It was not the alcohol that killed him,

it was his reflection which never left the glass,
not even as it fell and the whiskey carried him
across the floor. We found death to be a stain
we scrub from a shirt until the shirt is gone

·

What about death isn't a riddle?
A wolf slays a deer alongside a highway,

parts the ribs like a boy peering
through branches, and crawls inside.

First its head disappears.
Then the shoulders.

When I slow my car to the side of the road,
only its hind legs are kicking outside the body.

I walk toward the animals, now
a new, singular animal. Not split

but made by splitting, the body
thrashed open. I gaze inside to find

nothing but a citadel of nothing—bare
hide and ligaments—I speak

your single and holy name
into its belly. The sound rattled

like a spell. The sound grew
distant, and then it was gone.

The deer opened
its eyes.

THE CONSTRUCTION OF LIES AND MEMORY

There is a simple way
to begin: gather grass
and dust, beams and
beams of light or pine,
fire and smoke, the smell
of loam opening
like an orchard
after a good rain,
the monarchs lilting
above the bull thistle. A lie
is built as simply, as thin
and as delicate,
and it surrounds us
like the fields
two children might lie in
and gaze upward,
wondering if all that blue
is real, like the field
not far from my childhood
home, its small world
and smaller creek—where
I pulled crawfish carefully
from the reeds—so small
it is gone now, replaced
by grass, so small
my younger sister does not
remember it, so small it has
become a lie, I suppose,
but I'll gladly tell it. Gladly
hold it here and let you feel
its pincers, gentle at first

and then drawing the slightest
blood, a single drop
like a far off planet in the eye
of a telescope. Those years,
twenty years now
in the distance, also
the size of a planet
no one will ever touch;
a planet so far off it's not
even real, it couldn't be,
even if you were there once.
Even if when you turn
to stare upon it, until your eyes
widen and dry, it feels
almost as if it's staring back
and shimmers and blinks
like you, certain, but not.

RAIN

The rain has begun to fall, if I'm lucky
the fire will go out and you will follow, cross
my mind for a final time or at least take me

with you. The only way through is through.
If love is a city two people make then it is
also a place that has no use when its people leave,

though here I am tending to its dust. Nothing moves
but could. Even the city's single bird—birthed by our
laughter—sings a single note and that one note hangs

permanently in the air. This morning
I shot a bird with a gun not strong enough
to kill it. I wanted to watch it fail, I wanted

to steal the sky with a single curl
of my finger. I wanted to know
if what I want is ever what I want.

You were right. I'm not shit.
And you are gone.

SPOOL WEST

Last time I drove through Ohio,
I was headed east. The woman
I love still answered the phone.

Spaceman was still alive, John too.
I return home, driving west
along this unending spool of road,

the seam along which this country begins
to fray. I try to unstitch my one, singular life.
Even though it is yours, it never is

quite the one you want.
The engine works without knowing
why. I go on much the same—

I can almost fool myself into believing
I have become the machine. I stare
off into the shapeless fields

lost in the music of no music, only the hum.
I swear when I close my eyes I can still see
the road's pale glow, the median paint alive

with a million crushed seashells mixed in
with the paint. For a moment, it is all one
dark glittering wave curling beneath me.

I ride it out into the world, the unending
horizon dark and darkening. I almost believe
I could go on forever. Just like this.

V

THE STUDY OF DOORS AND KNOWING

if a single pupil devours the iris
if a black moon is discovered
inside each of our cells
if we lived in a kingdom of silence
if an aria were to rise splitting open
the boreal dark which darkens
if pain a gate pain a lake frozen
solid save its single eye widening
if sight begets sight
if eyes open across the body
if pain a sheet of paper incised
one stroke at a time
if fistfuls of night removed
like black hair from a drain
if each letter a wound
if we are all two people
and as we sleep we are
awake in another body
if that body dies
if we never sleep again
if I still feel the boy
inside me like a hunger
if each letter on the page
is a speck of his blood across snow
if each letter here could open
if we might crawl inside one now
if each vowel is the mouth
of a cave overlooking a new world
if we might dangle our feet over the edge

·

Boy who was himself a door, fifteen
red keyholes appearing wherever

the key fell, the way a shovel is a key
to the earth, though the boy never opens

wide enough to walk through, just enough
to see into the infinite rooms lit with planets gazing

back out, boy with a galaxy locked inside him.
Boy with blood black and shining, riddled

with stars. His blood ran from the house
and into the street where it continued

on to the sea, lifted into the sky and then
became it. Now there is a place in the Pacific

where it is always night.
His magnificent blood,

a wet universe gazing down on us.
His blood, an endless dream

lit by stars as it runs
from the keyholes opening

like fifteen eyes which see
forever.

LOOK

Passed Fredrikstad and Oslo, passed Tynset
and Røros, beyond villages so small
they take the names of the largest family

in town. I catch a glimpse of a house just beyond
the road. In its one lit window, a man stares
out, unmoving. His gaze a kind of shadow

wandering through dusk and into the hills.
To what? To his lover who is gone? To a life
which contains neither of them? I have looked

this way before at the woman I loved
the many times we parted at airports and
train stations until eventually we let go

and she did not look back. And if his eyes
then were stars above that nameless road
then I think they would be the last two to go out.

And though I can't say why, it is this gaze I carry
with me. Not the gaze of my mother or father
as they closed my bedroom door and watched

the dark fold over my face. Not the gaze
of my grandmother, dressed in a thin white light
and a hospital gown as she said my name and then

turned over toward the wall. Not the sick calf before
it was taken into the woods and shot. Not my childhood
dog before we drove her quietly to a quieter death.

Eventually, everything that can look will look
away, and our memory, which is a kind of faith,
will be unable to carry even itself.

SMOKE

His father, I hear, stays drunk,
refuses to die or can't

now. He lies awake listening
to his son who lives

now in the soft hum
of floodlights above

the court at night,
between the shuffle

of the shoes of boys
who are men now,

if even barely, who
learned to grow, somehow,

from a boy
who would be a boy

forever, a boy dissolving,
now smoke and smoke.

GLOMMA

The canoe glides through the river,
a single bolt of black lightning,

a comb sliding through the hair,
a tangled memory released.

One by one the orange lights
of farmhouses turn on

slowly, behind their windows,
each house wakes to look out

onto the river. Past
the breathing sill of the body,

past the one tractor still rumbling
across the dark field as it races

the first frost stirring just beyond the pines,
and the mining town with no mine now,

past the cattle and their bells, a steady music
so familiar the entire village came

to believe it was the stars
that were ringing.

ALONG THE SPENT HORIZON

The distance between us
                  and machines is less than we might think.

What animates metal is flesh,
                       what stops flesh is metal.

You should know where we're going,
                  where we have found ourselves again,

the simple and tired metaphor. The derricks dip
                  down across every landscape

toward the trembling crust of the earth, an arm
                  swinging as if possessed. Yes,

of course the earth is a body. Yes, it is his.
                  Yes, I'm tired of it too. Of so many things,

but in the long history of thieves,
                  no one is spared, least of all you or I,

dear reader. If you'll listen just a little longer,
                  I'd like to steal a few more moments

of your time and give you a small story:
                  A group of robbers run, smiling

but afraid, into the long night. The next morning
                  the shopkeeper lists what is missing:

Shoe polish, a locket without a face, a mirror
                              into which everyone who looks

is young again, defined suddenly
                              only by what is gone.

Let me say it this way instead and just once:
                              my friend is dead. There is no easy way

to explain everything that leads up to the end.
                              My grief sleeps, misshapen by rain,

beside the entrance to some lightless building.
                              I do not know the doorway

without it. I can't even remember
                              what's on the other side.

MIKKELS PLASS

I suppose it simply comes down to this: once I threw grass seed beside a river. I visited the plot each morning before stumbling half-awake to the barn where I would milk the cows for hours, dodging their hard, mud-caked tails. Soon after, the small green halms beginning to tremble in the breeze, a little more each morning as fog hid everything else, even my desire to leave, which carries me, I think. I visited so often the farmers named that small stretch of river *Mikkels Plass* or *Michael's Place*.

If nothing else, there is a small patch of grass along a river in Norway where children swim in the summer, where the water still carries winter in its melting starlight, and the Swedes come across the border to fish in their waist-high boots and not speak to each other as they flick their poles back and forth as if casting a spell.

I have tried this trick before, over water, and nothing.
Over a body stilled by time and still nothing.

Years before me there were others—before the Vikings and even before the Sami—and one of their stone tools lies in the wooden chest in the farmers' dining room like a secret heart, tilled up one spring years ago. This stone with its ancient line carved around the middle where the hilt of the tool would have been tethered makes its way into conversation over boiled potatoes and fish.

I know, you don't need to know any of this, but I have to tell you all the same, because I left that place, and I left this place here to get there, and I'll leave it again, and every summer is hot with my obsession to go, and I wake early, and tend to my gardens, and watch nothing change until it does.

Time flicks back and forth effortlessly and stretches out, un-spooled. The clock is a more complicated machine than the gun, and certainly the knife, but they all have the same final trick. There will, one day, be another war, and another, and the theory of everything comes down to grass and is simply grass, which grows long and green and endlessly. There are one hundred ways to destroy it, and there one hundred more ways it will find its way back out of the dirt.

FINALITY

For Don

I float home across the plains, over this dark thread
of road, past the lights along the Minnesota River—
golden nails fastening shut the horizon—past
the snow-covered fields reflecting the moon's wet light,
until we can no longer tell what is land
or water or sky, and we cannot tell
which our brother rests in now.
Everything to the east darkens
and the whole country closes
around the heart of the Midwest,
around its churches and its silos, its pilgrims
journeying before death to kneel and kiss
its winding fingers, its noble silence spreading
between the Mississippi and the Rust Belt like a moth-
torn quilt, a eulogy left unsaid at the edge
                                    of the lips. Death,
though it is final, is also hesitant and unsure.
It is the persistent silence which follows,
that convinces us this boy in the ground
was the one, this land too, these factories
and these barges sunning themselves in the grey light
as if they might dip beneath the water and re-emerge
glistening and alive; these docks and these cranes,
these warehouses angling into the shadows preserved
in a death-like geometry, though tenuous, as if
if we clap and summon the lord, if we stomp our
feet until we cannot smell what keeps the body
here, until the body shakes, then might these songs
wake him, might these factories turn and light
like a bulb screwed in, might we be sentence-like—

not final, but running on forever
through the grammar of mourning,
the grammar of laughter when laughter is all we have
left, until all that is left is his skin, and his bones,
and we who buried him are only stories or ash
on our grandchildren's mantels, and his name
spray painted on the Oak Park wall is painted over
or chips off and washes into the dirt, and his bones
too become earth, and the bullet
in his leg is all that remains and rests,
a small black seed opening in his coffin.

JOYOUS WORK

If there is a perfect joy it is similar
to a fever and begins somewhere

in the jowls then wings out like a hand
of cards thrust outward across a table.

I know, it has come over me. Once
in a silo 80-feet deep—I was

like a final breath working at the bottom
of a lung, leveling out hay dropped

from the claw sliding back and forth
along the rafters. I pitched my weight

for twelve hours, heaving the wet
grass how I have seen some drunk

men play the accordion at night
when they forget they own anything

at all and so, briefly, they don't.
Not even the music itself.

This work of the body
is the work of what? Not prayer,

that's too simple. Not dumb luck either.
No, it is more like an invocation left unsaid

when it swells and kicks in the body
like a frightened horse,

and it nearly burns, and we find there
are other ways to pray, like working the palms

raw, evening out a whole shorn field in a dark
tunnel piling to the top until, finally, you stand

on some unknown tons of hay and step
from the lip of the silo like a golden holy thing

and fly among the rafters, and it is your exhaustion
which carries you, which is for an instant

the single thing you own, and takes on the quality
of the spirit, which you are surprised to find

smells of wet grass, the cool rain outside,
the swallows roosting, and the grease

of the mechanical claw crying out, working
back and forth, a hard dark sea above you.

JUST YESTERDAY

Pain isn't worth any more than the words
              we can dig up to describe it.
                          Tell me of the sinew unspun

by metal, but make it pretty. Tell me
              of the collarbone tearing loose
                          from the skin like a branch,

but make it soft. Everyone wants
              us to spill poetically, in a way
                          that goes down easy—they want

us speak of maps by referring
              to their borders and not
                          by what's inside of them. I dreamt

you still named. I dreamt you
              naked. I dreamt you leaking
                          from time's advances. I dreamt

you siphoning out your own life
              through the needle, I dreamt
                        your spine crumbling like a palace

of cards, I dreamt every dead person
              I know was the same and lived
                        in the same cramped alley

of my skull. I'll tell you
              these stories until the words
                        materialize and I can stop

up a wound. I know,
                I might as well try
                                to gather the rain with a sieve,

but goddammit I need to try.
                I've been walking around
                                believing the dead

are like windows, this poem
                and other poems a hand full
                                of rocks. I want to shatter each

of your faces, O family, O friends,
                like you might walk out
                                from behind those gaps

in your smiles. Sometimes
                I hold a word to my ear
                                like a conch shell.

Sometimes I curse the ocean
                for what it cannot or will not say.
                                I surround these bodies

with sentence after sentence,
                and the words chant like a crowd,
                                the words become music,

the words become an orchestra of flies.
                I almost believe you will wake up,
                                all of you together.

I almost believe your name
        will slither its way back into
                your body and you will kick back

to life like a junkyard Cutlass,
        and you will walk out
                of your own funerals laughing.

How absurd, this choir
        of weeping, these caskets
                planted in the dirt like seeds.

It is so cold in this winter's lexicon,
        this language of nothing,
                of once was or never will be

again. Sometimes I want to kill
        my uncle for being
                a more miserable drunk than I was.

Sometimes I want him to die already
        so I can write about it;
                sometimes I too want to be a poem.

I don't want to be this pain,
        but the language used
                to unearth it. Sometimes

I curse archeologists
        for their basic tools telling us
                basic things. Sometimes

I think scientists are lazy. I too
        could dig a heart out of a chest,
                but what do any of them know

about pulling the history from a body
        without killing it? Just yesterday
           scientists discovered a new ligament

in the human knee. Just yesterday
        I found out I can't sleep
           for a whole new set of reasons.

Just yesterday I wrote and wrote
        and wrote and kept writing.
           I've committed to not killing anyone,

especially myself. Just yesterday.
        I found new ways to say
           I miss you, my god
                how I miss you all.

SECONDLY. FINALLY

Who tells your story now, heaven-faced boy?
Sometimes I fear I may have killed you

a second time, how silence is a kind of death,
how having your story told for you

is also a kind of death. Secondly, finally,
I continue to begin with the end

as if that's all there is, as if
that's where your story began, bled into

the world through your own wounds.
Somedays I feel I have taken on your shadow

and am the appropriator of your aunt's
grief, which is dull and silent

like a round stone in the shoe
as it works its way into the skin and will

eventually, through the blood, become
a part of the body, a knob or handle in the bone,

as if this grief could open us,
a skeleton, a screen door, a bolt

of silk unraveling. My memory of you
cinches tight and I tell the story

from the beginning. This time
you are alive. This time, I say nothing.

THE MIDDLE PLACE

Etched along each roof,
the slender, serrated teeth

of the sky: the lord's still
mouth caught one the eaves.

Every frozen thing starves.
Stray dogs forage in the trash,

the cat's carcass, there since
October, rests against the fence,

small tufts rising through the snow
like grey weeds. Though still,

in the darkening, small lights gold as yarrow.
Maybe it's just the street lamps, a few

triumphant stars, or my own
yearning cast off the television

by the dumpster, jumper cables
snaking out of the shattered screen

as though someone tried to revive
the myths we live by. Here

in the long night of the north, we survive
on recollection alone. I am, when I close

my eyes—just slightly, thin as keyholes—
a child again, spying on the distant life

of my elders on the other side of the living-
room door. If I stay here for a moment,

just like this, I think I can catch each
of their gazes as they pass over me—

like the headlights of a single car passing
at midnight, a smooth gloved hand sliding

across the walls as it goes—and if I squint
even tighter, I think I can keep them

with me just a little longer. I can see the light
by which each of my memories is lit:

the trembling halo above my grandmother
twenty years ago as she harvests

raspberries alongside the dirt road.
Her hands redden also like light until

the light goes out, and my grandfather
sings at his piano in the dark

until his voice goes hoarse.
He cannot remember the words.

He cannot find the keys. If I can
do anything, it is this: carry a small flame

back into my memory and let them
warm their hands beside it.

DECAY AND MORE DECAY

For my final wish, another
final wish. The end

is a kind of current.
You could light

a whole city
on what is gone.

A last breath
stirs the pages

of finished books
on the mantel gathering

dust; our skin lifts
off then settles.

For my final trick,
a final trick: the heart

working in mundane
ways. Each time

you touch anyone
there is a chance

your atoms will move
in unison, parting,

and your hand
will pass through

their body and become
lodged there

in the jaw or behind
the breast. Of course,

this doesn't happen,
but the thought of it

almost makes my finger
running across a naked

spine in candlelight feel
dangerous, and permanent

in this danger, like you
might remember this,

and I might love you
more in that moment

than the moment
we let go, parting,

slipping by one another
into the cold night, but it is

the night that parts,
wide and shivering.

NOTES

The first section of "The Study of Words and Heaven" draws its inspiration from a conversation with Michael Bazzett.

The line "what's a little more pain when pain's eternal" in the poem "out there" is a line taken from the first section of Matt Rasmussen's poem "Elegy in X parts".

ACKNOWLEDGMENTS

Sincere thanks is owed to the editors of the following publications in which some of these poems first appeared, often in different form.

The Adroit Journal: "Finality", "Look"

BOAAT Journal: "The Insomniac Maps the Night"

The Carolina Quarterly: "The Pill", the "Self-Erasure as Applied to My Memory" series appeared as a single poem by the same name

The Collagist: "And"

Copper Nickel: The first section in "The Study of Knives and Music" appeared as a single poem titled "A History of the Knife"

Drunk In a Midnight Choir: The first section of "The Study of Doors and Knowing" appeared as a single poem titled "IF"

Hayden's Ferry Review: The third section of "The Study of Knives and Music" appeared as a single poem titled "When Your Friend Is Killed While Talking on the Phone"

Ninth Letter: "Secondly. Finally", the second section of "The Study of Doors and Knowing" appeared as a single poem titled "The Blade as Key"

Phoebe: "The Law of Halves as Applied to the Blade"

Poetry Northwest: The first section of "The Study of the Dead and Puzzles" appeared as a single poem titled "Refraction"

Prime Number: "Sound Lost in the North"

Redivider: The final section of "Study of the Dead and Puzzles" appeared as a single poem titled "Aggregate"

Secondly. Finally, a short chapbook containing several of these poems, was published by *Organic Weapon Arts* in April, 2015.

"At the Lake" was anthologized in Best New Poets 2018.

Additional thanks and eternal gratitude is owed for the support, time, and space provided to me by the LOFT Literary Center, the Minnesota State Arts Board, the Metropolitan Regional Arts Council, the Bread Loaf Writers' Conference, the Key West Literary Seminar, and the Lanesboro Artist Residency Program. This book could not have been completed without the generous assistance from each of these wonderful organizations.

Thank you, Button. From the first camera at CUPSI to this book, my work has been championed. Hanif, Dylan, and of course Sam. From our many travels, readings, conversations, and debates, you have a long hand reaching across my work. Thank you for asking again and again if I was working on a book and for making it real.

Thank you to my teachers: Jamaal May, Terrance Hayes, Rowan Ricardo Phillips, Tarfia Faizullah, Steve Seidel, Professor Sara Lawrence-Lightfoot, my sister V., Eve Ewing, and Dan Mrozowski. My middle and high school English teachers for seeing I was a poet before I did and making sure I did not forget it, especially Mr. Zelle, Mr. Woolman, and of course Michael Bazzett whose guidance and friendship has been ever-present for the past sixteen years. Your classes restored my wonder in literature, the world, and my understanding of my place in both.

My sweet, sweet friends, space makers, peers, coaches, and comrades whom I love so deeply. Thank you for your edits, conversation, support, validation, vision, and friendship: Donovan, Danez, Cam, Sam S., Paul, Tish, Camonghne, Khary, Clint, Anders, Deonte, Rachel my mother hen, Riley & Ryan and the CUPSI teams, Allison and Mike and the MPLS team. My KWLS sisters, what a gift to grow together, momma Sara, my sister, cousin, frand Dantiel—get fed. Thank you. My family Chace and T., how

I love you both. MWWP. A.M.L forever, you guide me even when we're far apart. The First-Five, Shanae, Toni, Andrea, and Vaughan, where would I be without you? Forever my sisters. Ola, always my love, always my admiration and gratitude. Heather L.M. and Anthony Martinez, your selfless, unquestioned support. My fellow Bread Loaf waiters, especially Matt, Monica, Kathryn, Edgar, and Keith—get fed. Brorene og søsterene mine i Norge, takk. Eg er glad i dere og eg tenker på dere ofte, men vi ses snart da. My many chosen families who have loved me so and championed my work, the Ellisons and Smiths especially, to my youth work families: Bryce, Ms. Elaine, Zayed, Gwen, Ryan, Donnell, Vi, Katie, Qamar, Kelly, Rocki, Makeda, Zach, Sue, Amy S., Pattie, Kowanna, Auntie Akani, Ms. Pearly, Jessie, Esha, Princess, I am so loved and have learned to love harder and better because of you each. That capacity for love has informed my work deeply.

My dearest Hieu Minh Nguyen, whose love, patience, care, and wisdom has touched nearly every poem in this book. These past nine years have been better and softer because of you. And of course to my brother Jeremiah Ellison. My first reader and last reader, whose unflinching belief in my work, and whose expansive imagination, wonder, rigorous expectations and rigorous love has kept me moving forward for half my life. Who would I be without you?

And of course, finally, to my family. To all of you, but especially my sisters who put up with me, believed in me amidst the chaos, and called every Friday evening for years to make sure I was going to my meetings. Thank you. To mom and dad, I got the better end of this deal. Thank you for patience, your tough love, your soft love, your never-ending love. Mom, for reading to me every night as a boy, stretching my imagination and teaching me to love stories and words. Dad, for listening to my endless ramblings and tall tales as a child, teaching me my stories were worthy of being listened to. Grandma, for holding us all together.

I'm sorry, there are so many who should be listed here. Please charge my head and not my heart.

I don't deserve any of you. Thank you.

MICHAEL LEE is a Norwegian-American writer, youth worker, and organizer. He has received grants and scholarships from the Minnesota State Arts Board, the LOFT Literary Center, and the Bread Loaf Writers' Conference. Winner of the Scotti Merrill Award for poetry from the Key West Literary Seminar, his poetry has appeared in *Ninth Letter, Hayden's Ferry Review, Indiana Review, Poetry Northwest, Copper Nickel,* and the *Best New Poets Anthology,* among others. Michael has worked as a dishwasher, a farmhand, a teaching artist, a social studies teacher, a case manager for youth experiencing homelessness, and he currently manages a youth program using food as a tool for health, wealth, and social change. He works, lives, writes, organizes, and dreams in North Minneapolis, spending his free time reading books and working in his garden.

OTHER BOOKS BY BUTTON POETRY

If you enjoyed this book, please consider checking out some of our others, below. Readers like you allow us to keep broadcasting and publishing. Thank you!

Neil Hilborn, *Our Numbered Days*
Hanif Abdurraqib, *The Crown Ain't Worth Much*
Olivia Gatwood, *New American Best Friend*
Donte Collins, *Autopsy*
Melissa Lozada-Oliva, *peluda*
Sabrina Benaim, *Depression & Other Magic Tricks*
William Evans, *Still Can't Do My Daughter's Hair*
Rudy Francisco, *Helium*
Guante, *A Love Song, A Death Rattle, A Battle Cry*
Rachel Wiley, *Nothing Is Okay*
Neil Hilborn, *The Future*
Phil Kaye, *Date & Time*
Andrea Gibson, *Lord of the Butterflies*
Blythe Baird, *If My Body Could Speak*
Desireé Dallagiacomo, *SINK*
Dave Harris, *Patricide*

Available at buttonpoetry.com/shop and more!